Occasionally
I Contemplate
Murder

*To the poor target
of the one who probably
triggered this book.*

Occasionally
I Contemplate
Murder

Stefan Stenudd

arriba.se

Stefan Stenudd is a Swedish author, historian of ideas, artist, and a long-time instructor in the peaceful martial art aikido. He has published a number of books in Sweden as well as English, both fiction and non-fiction.

Among the latter is an interpretation of the Chinese classic *Tao Te Ching* and the Japanese samurai classic *Go Rin no Sho* by Miyamoto Musashi. His novels explore existential subjects from Stone Age drama to science fiction, but lately stay more and more focused on the present. He has also written some plays for the stage and the screen. In the history of ideas he studies the thought patterns of creation myths, as well as Aristotle's *Poetics*. He has his own extensive website:
www.stenudd.com

Also by Stefan Stenudd:
Tao Te Ching. The Taoism of Lao Tzu Explained, 2011.
Cosmos of the Ancients. The Greek Philosophers on
Myth and Cosmology, 2007, 2011.
Life Energy Encyclopedia, 2009.
Aikido Principles, 2008.
Qi. Increase Your Life Energy, 2008.
Attacks in Aikido, 2008.
Aikibatto. Sword Exercises for Aikido Students, 2007.
Your Health in Your Horoscope. Introduction to Medical Astrology, 2009.

Fiction:
Occasionally I Contemplate Murder, 2006, 2011.
All's End, 2007.

Occasionally I Contemplate Murder.
(Previously published with the title *Murder*.)
Copyright © Stefan Stenudd, 2006, 2011.
Cover, photos, and book design by the author.
All rights reserved.
ISBN 978-91-7894-050-9
Publisher: Arriba, Malmö, Sweden, info@arriba.se
www.arriba.se

Welcome!

This world is, I find, a strange place to be, wherein my brain is not the best of guides.

Somehow, somewhere in the very core of my being, I believe myself to understand all as clear as day. I really do.

But that's in the core, a centre unreachable, hidden inside layer upon layer of misconceptions. My conscious mind is lost.

It's like an onion. Rip off the peels, one after the other, until you reach the centre — only to find it empty. No nut, not a thing to explain all those peels, covering the kitchen sink and making you weep.

Yes, the onion contains the secret of the universe. I dare say that the onion *is* the secret of the universe.

You can reveal it with tools of the hand and of the mind. It doesn't even take very hard work. But you find nothing, and it sure makes you cry.

It's all very logical, I guess. If you take the peels away, if you dig down to the very core — well, then it's no longer a core of anything. So it's nothing. What else could it be?

Where's a poor human being, the biggest brain among primates, to find guidance?

So, occasionally I contemplate murder.

Not only the centre of the onion is empty. Practically everything is, our science tells us.

If you look really close at things, there are atoms, of course. But they don't fill up the space, shoulder to shoulder, like an American football team does right before play-off. Not at all. They are as sparse as the planets around our sun, as the stars in the Milky Way.

From a distance, the stars seem to be crowded, but there are vast distances between them. Well, think of it:

They're so far apart that wherever in this universe you may happen to stand watching, there's never more than one of them looking any larger to your eyes than the usual dot of white light. Well, unless you're in the vicinity of a twin star system. Binoculars make no difference — not even the largest telescope.

Dots of white light, forever.

You can measure the moon and the sun, and an oak growing on the other side of the field — for example with a pen held straight out in front of you, like artists do. Not the stars. The stars are so far away that they're infinitesimal from our viewpoint.

One could say that we don't actually see them. Our eyes just register their light. If all those lights were switched off, we'd have no way at all of detecting the existence of the stars.

Then we'd really be alone. Just us, our sun, and a few neighboring planets. That would be it.

Maybe it is.

I once had such a theory. This is it:

Perhaps there's just one solar system — ours — and the rest is an optical illusion. I'm not altogether sure, but I think it's possible. At least it's not as absurdly unthinkable as one might at first assume.

Check it out:

If there's only our solar system, and nothing but emptiness all around it — as if a Creator God was a very lazy fellow — then gravity would make all the light from the sun return to it, eventually.

Light, whatever it is, obeys the laws of gravity, we've learned. So, if no other mass existed in the universe but the one in our sun and its protégés, then the light would have to return.

All the rays of light would return a little differently — because of the small changes in gravitational pull, the particular direction each beam of light started with, and so forth.

Our planets move in their separate orbs. The sun, too, behaves a bit irregularly. Given the time it would take a beam of light to turn and return, those small disturbances might very well make the sum of light beams give the impression of a cosmos full of stars. Yet, they're all mere reflections of the one and only star, which is our sun.

This is not the case, of course, but some time ago I found the idea intriguing.

I guess that the most prosperous line of analysis would be to explore, not the very idea, but the reasons behind my interest in it.

The astronomical perspective is intriguing — for what it probably is, as well as for what it's most definitely not.

What is true, though, is the emptiness.

Although the combined magnitude of the stars of the universe is impressive, they surely are sparse as police officers in nighttime subway trains, when you consider all the space they have at their disposal.

Think about it! All those distances, presumably impenetrable by anyone and anything but light itself.

This is a universe of loneliness immense.

Not only space is as empty as the core of the onion.

Let's turn our attention to what mass and matter there is.

It's hard, for sure, when a golf ball hits your head or you have your car's bumper ram the side of your neighbor's brand new Mercedes. But a closer look reveals it as being filled with nothing.

Tiny atoms separated by distances that are quite comparable, relatively, to those of the stars in space. Not even in the hardest and heaviest of substances do they have any reason to feel crowded.

Even the very atom itself — that little rascal, too, is mainly nothing at all. Nothingness with a number of names to it.

Our increasing terminology indicates that the more we search, the less we find. The atom is an emptiness ruled by tensions and attractions yet to be understood.

When you take a closer look, there's quite a lot yet to be understood. A lot of nothings.

Of course, the universe is really but an idea, a concept that would not withstand serious scrutiny. Whatever we succeed to penetrate, we're met with the same elusive emptiness.

When examined more closely, the universe seems to be a work of side-scenes only. Like the cinema: beautiful colors, but nothing behind the screen.

Whoever got the idea of the universe obviously didn't give it much thought.

We should be very careful, when trying to scrutinize our cosmos. Who knows, if we succeed, if we have a major breakthrough, we might just blow it all. Like a soap bubble, when touched by the fingertip of a curious child.

Maybe that's what it is about. To blow it all. The meaning of life.

So, occasionally I contemplate murder.

In this world of contradiction and confusion, murder is something quite substantial. Nevertheless, I must mention that it's not the kind of contemplation I altogether approve of.

Some of its aspects I would proclaim in the largest and most mixed of crowds, without hesitation. Others, though, are a bit delicate. Still, definitely interesting.

Those lines of thought aren't always encouraging. On the other hand, what lines of thought are?

When scrutinized carefully, our world seems to have a number of flaws. One wouldn't have too hard a time coming up with ideas for improving it.

Anyway, that's not a waterproof reason for condemning it.

There are many aspects of murder. The very first question may be: how can people at all be able to kill each other?

If we're to give the theory of evolution any credibility, we must ponder this some. Why would a species come up with, and seemingly forever keep, the habit of killing among its own? In a world full of dangers, it must be regarded as overdoing things.

I mean, would a parachutist let himself fall as close to the ground as the laws of aerodynamics allow him, before it's of fatal necessity to pull the string?

Would a diver stay underwater until he has sucked the last breath of oxygen from his tubes, and would a motorcyclist enter a curve of the road with the maximum speed he believes himself able to handle?

Yes, they would.

Darwin must have missed something. If the strongest instinct of any species is to protect itself from extinction, then mankind acts from a malady, which must surely have had all the chances to be deleted by evolution.

It's a paradox, a most disturbing anomaly of Darwinism, that a species would fondle such dangerous habits. Yet, we obviously do.

Darwin himself might have stated that murder is yet another way of the species, however risky, to accomplish the survival of the fittest. Still I wonder, is it really the fittest that holds the knife, and the less fitting who momentarily sheathes its sharp blade in his own flesh?

Indeed I doubt it, if we're not to regard the murderer as the fittest by virtue of his deed alone.

Well, all the princes of the Renaissance would certainly cheer in accordance with such a system of merit. As Mussolini, a somewhat misplaced member of their community, reasoned:

Whoever gets the power has thereby proven his right to it.

Perhaps he who takes the lives of others

thereby proves the right to his own? It's the law of the bully, the supremacy of the savage.

Some of us would certainly be attracted to such a world, and it definitely makes good action movies.

If nothing else, a savage kingdom could be sort of sexy.

Wouldn't such an order of things start a messy rally around the world!

And one day, there he'd stand, the very prime of mankind. Screaming like Conan the Barbarian, with bloodstained hands stretching towards the sky, and his feet sunk knee-deep into a mount of corpses.

Hail the ultimate man!

How come he hears no praise?

No, it doesn't work like that. Murder has got nothing to do with evolution.

Death, on the other hand, probably does. Death has many roles. But murder, no. Nature didn't invent it, nor did any God. Man did.

Sort of.

I wonder what it's like to be murdered.

Well, I'm not overly familiar with any kind of dying — neither when inflicted by the will of a fellow human being, nor the dying by what is called natural causes. Certainly, all of it is intriguing.

Murder in particular — how does it feel to be its victim?

There's one important difference between death from disease, old age, or by accident, on the one hand, and death by murder on the other.

The so-called natural means of departure are quite self-explanatory. Mostly one is well prepared for them, although probably never enough.

In an accident, death may certainly be as sudden and surprising as a truck blocking the way immediately behind a turn of the road. Either you have time to perceive what obstacle you run into, in which case no further questions need answering, or you don't, in which case there's no question at all.

Any which way, it's not a mystery.

Murder, on the other hand, gives birth to so many more questions insisting on being answered — if you're given the time. Who did it? And why? Why!

I may find in my mind the reason for what is done to me, or it may be outspokenly given to me by my bane — something I doubt that any murderer would supply, unless he thereby attempts to gain the determination needed to complete his deed. If that's the case, he will not succeed.

However, no matter how the murder is explained to me, still my mental ordeal isn't over. Not nearly.

What time I have left of conscious reasoning, I'll spend rapidly going over and over what actions of mine would have prevented this outcome. What had I done wrong? Why couldn't my bane and I have found some less definite solution?

And what kind of life will this deed prepare for my assassin? Will the murder really work to his advantage, even in the long run?

With all these questions in my mind, I would probably make this my most important transition in a state of utmost frustration.

Or would I become like a saint and think first to forgive my murderer, like the heroes of both long gone and modern day legends always do?

Methinks — as long as it does not cancel his reservation in one or other hell — I'll be glad to forgive.

Don't punish my assassin, said the dying king Gustaf III of Sweden, when shot at the masquerade of the Opera, in 1792. Did he seriously believe they'd ever let that captain of the army, who had fired his gun into the king's abdomen, walk away a free man, to be punished in this earthly life only by his own conscience?

If the king had been convinced that his subjects would obey his last command — would he still have made it?

Unlike modern day bullets, the small pieces of lead in captain Anckarstrom's pistol hit so inaccurately, it took the king two weeks to die. He had time to ponder the murder.

Yet, it's not a very agreeable state of mind to be in, at the moment of leaving one's mortal coil: frustration, and maybe bitter thoughts of vengeance.

Perhaps there are no ghosts at all. But if there are, I can think of no better melting pot for them than people being the fatal victims of worldly plots of their fellow men.

If there is such a thing as a soul, how can it possibly turn away from an event this traumatic, to enter the eternal tranquility of the hereafter?

One cannot go without some peace of mind.

Is it possible for the victim of a murder to come to peace with it, gracefully succumb to the laws of biology, and leave? If he cannot — what kind of death will that be?

One should be prepared for death in whatever shape it appears.

Some people die, and really live to tell about it. Do they have wonderful tales!

Now and then, people die for a while, but are brought back by medical effort or something else. Generally, they just wake up from a big black nothing, and that's it.

But during that period of non-being, a few do have vivid experiences, which seem to be similar in every case.

They pass out, but somehow they're not unconscious. Instead, their minds commence a marvelous voyage.

Brought out of their body, they watch it for a time and feel very estranged. Then they enter a long tunnel of light, traveling through it with incomprehensible speed. At the end of this tunnel, someone approaches them — a loving, splendorous being.

Well, a kind of Jesus.

This kind of Jesus speaks gently to them, not exactly by words, and helps them review their whole lives. From start to finish, in every little detail. Nothing is omitted.

It must be an overwhelming experience, possible only in a state of non-being.

Myself, I feel that I would surely explode from such a rerun. I cannot withstand the force of my memories in any quantity.

All the time of life lived, sometimes joyous, sometimes not, luring behind me. It is simply too much.

Beautiful, yes, but too much.

Well, sometimes in their past, those momentary guests in death's domain behaved somewhat improperly. Reviewing such incidents, they're embarrassed before the kind of Jesus.

He is of a very understanding and forgiving nature, though. It seems that the only punishment they get for their evil — or mostly just stupid — deeds, is that moment of embarrassment: to view their so-called sin together with such a witness, and to feel shame.

But really, that's a punishment severe enough to make the most cynical of sinners, the most horrible of perverted psychopaths, bow his head and repent.

Think of it!

Many of my memories are so unpleasant to my conscience that I dare not face them even in the discretion of my own mind's solitude.

To have them shared, as clearly as were they relived, with a wondrous being of light and love, in that very domain which is the border between life and something else — that must surely be a purgatory as hot as any fire.

One needs to be forgiven.

I wonder, which one of my sins will then cause me the most embarrassment?

I don't see that I've committed plenty of evil deeds. However, even if my actions have not been overly savage, might they have been as sinful in intent as any beastly brutality?

I guess that I will feel the guiltiest about those deeds where I was the least unaware.

Calculation is the most compromising. To plan and execute a deed, fully wishing for the consequences of it. In cold blood, we call it.

Blood should not be cold.

One incident immediately comes to mind. Although not nearly the most deplorable thing I've done, nor very uncommon, the memory of it harasses me.

This is it:

When I was about twelve years of age, a friend of mine and I put my cat in a canvas bag, hooked the bag to a coat hanger, and started throwing tennis balls at it.

The cat was fighting to get out, but not for long.

Soon enough, the cat fell still inside the bag, while the balls were hitting at it. I think we threw them as hard as we were able to.

A strange intermezzo. I'm sure that the cat wondered what it was all about. Us boys did, too. But oh, such lust was involved in throwing those balls!

What stopped us was not really our conscience, but embarrassment from the great pleasure it induced in us. Pleasure of any size tends to intimidate us human beings.

Also, the cat was very smart to lie still. We began to worry that we had seriously wounded it.

When we finally let the cat out of the bag, it was quite unharmed — at least physically. The canvas of the bag was so thick, it must have offered the cat a good enough protection, I keep telling myself.

While we were still throwing the balls, I noticed that my friend was glaring at me.

I must confess that I threw them with much more enthusiasm than he did. Partly, but only partly, because the cat belonged — if such a word can at all be used about a cat, or about any living creature — to my family.

Well, my friend glared pensively, puzzled to find such a compulsion in me.

His eyes, so clear and penetrating, I still remember vividly. He was a witness.

Although not exactly a kind of Jesus, his presence made my deed much more embarrassing to me — at the time of it, and ever since.

Still, I'm convinced that the kind of Jesus

will find much more tender spots in my conscience. I would too, of course, if I made an honest attempt.

I do not.

People who have been to a short visit in that mysterious beyond, return with the impression that there is one firm rule.

Although the kind of Jesus tends to let bygones be bygones, there are two deeds he doesn't take that gently: murder and suicide.

His aversion to murder isn't difficult to understand. It's not an invention of Gods, but of men. Sort of.

As a matter of fact, this deed is a way of men's intervention with the very schemes of the Gods. So, of course they don't take it lightly.

But suicide? Why can't they accept suicide?

Man is given freedom of choice, and sometimes a hell of a place to execute it. Some of us aren't really apt to it and wish to leave.

I mean, not every kid at the amusement park wants to ride the roller coaster.

When you think about it, some kids don't want to ride it — and others not only want to, with all their hearts, but they release the seat belt, stand up in the carriage, and do just about everything to induce a fatal accident.

It's a strange kind of game, popular among some of the wildest boys — the daredevil fever.

What's their wish?

Some years ago, there was a hobby spreading among teenage boys in Stockholm, Sweden. They rode the subway trains, not in the carriages but between them, standing on the iron connections. Not too much room, and hardly a comfortable ride.

Now and then, a kid would slip and fall.

It was not even a way of getting a free ride. It must have been a wish for the final departure.

A young friend of mine had another way of treating his life disrespectfully.

At the age of eighteen, he had a baby with his equally young girlfriend. He was mighty proud and fully prepared to dedicate the rest of his years to the well-being of this child.

It seems that his girlfriend had other plans. She kicked him out of their apartment, suddenly indifferent to his love and care.

A few weeks later, the baby died.

For no apparent medical reason. Such things do happen, although rarely. Sudden Infant Death, they call it. The kid just let go of its life, and the doctors could do nothing to retrieve it.

That's when my friend lost his respect for life.

He fell into a depression. A strange kind of depression, in such a way that he was always able to talk about it.

He spoke ironically, almost self-mockingly, about how sad his life had become, how impossible it was for him to feel happy. No hope. And he smiled while telling me.

It became as casual as any conventional greeting:

How are you today? Just rotten, thank you.

Of course it bothered me, but the fact that he readily talked about it made consoling him much more difficult than had he not. What to say to somebody who knows all too well what's wrong?

That's life.

Increasingly, he showed signs of treating life the same way his infant son had done — letting it go.

He drank some, hung around some, and nothing happened. Now and then, he made half-hearted approaches to girls his age, but soon retreated. He would not let life get a firm grip on him again, wouldn't let anything tempt him into renewed enthusiasm.

He began mistreating his body in such a way that he stumbled around even when only mildly drunk. Never watching his step, not showing the least care for his own person.

He rapidly became what is called accident-prone. Soon enough, the accident arrived.

At a party, when he opened the window to throw some beer up, he lost his balance and fell.

The apartment was three stories up. My young friend hit the ground — not hard enough to die, but enough to become severely crippled, stuck to a wheelchair for the rest of his life. He can still show his broad grin, but not much more of the body obeys him.

Yet, he keeps on making jokes about it all.

I wonder why he didn't die. Didn't he want to, was he ambiguous about it?

Somehow, I get the feeling that he crippled his body to this extent, just to disable it as a tool for suicide, were he ever to succumb to that wish.

Yes, maybe that's it. Maybe he never seriously considered suicide, deep inside, but was so wary of the risk of one day reconsidering, that this was his method to prevent it. He was disarming himself.

Well, it worked. Not only has he made it next to impossible to execute the necessary steps for committing suicide, but he has also found immediate everyday problems to occupy his mind.

It's not happiness, I guess. Still, it works pretty well, so far.

That's life.

Jesus, the very prophet to insist on walking straight to Golgotha, although well aware of the outcome — should not he find it in his heart to tolerate suicide? Even to respect it.

It's a thing to pity. But to punish?

On the other hand, looking at it from the viewpoint of the Gods, I can see the reason for their intolerance. To them, suicide is nothing but murder.

Of course it is. If we are the handicraft of a Creator God, and He is our father, then we're killing children of His, even if it is ourselves.

To Him, it makes no difference whose hand performs the stabbing — a life of His creation is taken.

Our free will, the conscious mind, is something other than the living body. If not altogether expelled from the bosom of our Creator God, the conscious mind is at least separated from it.

By the same line of reasoning the body is not.

Therefore, strictly speaking, in so-called suicide, a stranger is forcing his will upon the innocent body, the God child, who has no say in it.

One must admit, no matter how decided the conscious mind is to commit suicide, the body never agrees.

So, in the perspective of a Creator God, it is murder.

God is firm. Don't mess with His children.

I would appreciate His concern more, though, if He could be just a trifle preventive. That's no more than any other parent tries to be.

Oh, Mighty One, where are you when we really need you?

Coming to think of it — where are you?

Maybe murder is, in essence, an act of revolt against the Gods — a demonstration of disagreement. Men might do it to consciously interfere with the heavenly order of things, and get some kind of kick out of it.

Although the Gods disapprove, they don't let their aversion lead to any kind of action against us while we're in this earthly coil. They might accuse us in the hereafter, when the deed is irrevocably done, but they don't put a stop to murder.

Maybe murder is a kind of puberty, a period in the development of mankind, necessary to go through. Can it be like one of the Freudian stages? Anal, oral, genital — and mortal.

If baby insists on playing with his little penis, a sensible parent knows not to stop him, or baby will stay forever in a state of compulsion to do just that. Could it be that we need to kill each other, now and then, to be at all able to overcome this compulsion?

In that case — for how long?

Murder is a tricky business. It seems to be the most difficult to pull through the first time around. But those who have the experience admit that it gets easier every time it is repeated.

Man is an adaptive beast. The act of murder can easily become more and more of an addiction.

Addiction is a strange thing. It comes only to habits that are bad and harmful. Or does indulgence, the gluttony of it, turn everything into harmful substance? A metamorphosis induced by quantity.

Well, there are people who believe that diluting substances changes them completely, so why not the other way around? Anything nutritious must be poisonous in too large or concentrated a dosis.

I've heard that even plain water is poisonous, if you drink too much of it. There was a woman in France who committed suicide by drinking forty liters of water.

Even air makes you dizzy, if you inhale rapidly and forcefully. And if you don't inhale enough, that gets you, too.

Life is a delicate balance.

The addiction of murder involves a great deal of pleasure. The mass murderer gets some kind of satisfaction from ending the lives of others. Putting a stop to life spans, he forces the irrevocable onto his victims, and by that indeed provokes the Gods.

It's not hard to conceive the thrill of it all. We've been hunters for millions of years, guarding the survival of our species through the reluctant death of other beasts. What prey is more of a challenge than man himself?

To kill others must also be a way of playing with that irresistible force, which is sure one day to hit oneself.

I can't avoid death, cannot keep it off — but I can speed up its arrival to others as well as to myself. By invoking death I pretend to control it and get a little more used to facing it.

Yes, that can be satisfying.

Watch him, my fellow human being — breathing, shivering, and widening his eyes in terror, at the moment of the blow. See blood and agony, see his knees bend and the whole body sink to the ground. Then, he is no more.

Whatever that may be.

It's exciting like nothing, nothing else, to be the catalyst of such an event. Making the dark mystery of death a swift tool in one's own hand.

Therefore, I'm not sure that the laissez-faire strategy of the Gods, if that's the case, is the wisest line of action. By allowing us to indulge in murder, instead of us getting fed up with it, they might make us forever addicted.

Is that what's happening?

Not so many of us commit murder, and not as often as in past days, we're led to assume. However, when we do, we tend to think in a larger scale than yesteryears. Also, we develop ever more efficient equipment for it.

Murder easily becomes a hobby, a habit, whatever the reason proclaimed for it. We excel at coming up with reasons.

Summing things up, we seem to do a twisted kind of progress. On the other hand — we never really stop playing with our penises, either.

On the conceptual as well as on the practical level, murder can be exciting.

In past times it was quite a messy business, of course. The murderer was never farther away from his victim than for the spilled blood also to stain him.

That's no longer the case.

Except for the traditional kinds of killing, used solely by those of primitive taste or lacking in means, there's a multitude of methods, not requiring the murderer to be closer to his victim than the distance that can be traversed by a rifle's bullet. That's quite a distance.

Like most things in our technological society, murder has become a mere pressing of buttons. Something abstract. The hardship of it is banished from everything but the murderer's own imagination.

On the other hand, I guess it has always been precisely the imagination that tormented every murderer the most.

In this aspect, killing is somewhat like dying. It's not the moment of the event that's so scary, but the time thereafter — God knows how long.

What's it like on the other side of the event? The perspective is vertiginous to both participants alike. What's it like, the land of death — and the remaining life of the one who caused it?

That uncertainty is shared equally by the victim and his bane.

Even if the memory of the deed torments the murderer's mind for no other reason than his expectation and fear of such agony — the pain is no less real.

The mind is a devilish trap.

Still, many a man is fully capable of risking the incurable malady for some reason or other.

Frequently, the reason appears to be ridiculous insignificant. Indeed, it seems that people find it much harder to bear with minute irritations, than with the grand injustices.

Whatever the weight of the cause, many do take the step in spite of our mysterious fear.

Why?

Is it the temptation of sin, of anything utterly taboo? It's hard, very hard, to withstand the impulse of doing something horrible.

Fear is an attractive, seductive brew. Who wants not to taste catastrophe?

The only thing one really has to do is to trick one's self-protective instincts into believing that there's a good chance of getting away with it.

That's an easy task.

Murder is an expression of power, ultimate power.

Man can do many things — construct bridges, split the atom, and walk on the moon. Still, no other power is as infinite, as divine, as these two: to give life, and to take it.

So, of course they are related. The two opposing ends of a line. Could it be in this relation that we may find an explanation as to how murder is at all possible?

Think of it:

We reproduce in such a fashion, man and woman, that we're led to believe we are the creators of new life. It really seems as if we're making our offspring, all by ourselves.

Well, if the birth of a human being is nothing but the joining of an egg and a sperm, then I guess we do have the right to call ourselves creators. Unto our offspring, we are the Gods.

For sure, we frequently treat our children in such a manner and demand of them to treat us accordingly. Creator and creation.

Then, if we regard ourselves as the makers of life, we naturally feel entitled to be the ones breaking it, as well. We start lives, so we end them, too. It makes obvious sense.

If we didn't see reproduction as an accomplishment of our own, it would probably be extremely difficult for us to consider murder, even more so to commit it.

We are the victims of unavoidable hubris.

Maybe this state of affairs makes us feel entitled, yes, quite obliged to end lives as frequently as we commence them. In search of balance.

In fact, if we can be accused of actually ending lives in the act of murder, then we must be said to start them in intercourse. We are worth as much praise for the latter, as we're given blame for the former.

Balance.

Murder is magic, as is life. It takes two to make a baby, whether or not that making is the real act of creation. It also takes two, evidently, to commit murder: the killer and the victim.

One could regard the act of murder as a kind of rape, enforcing the will of one upon the other. A rape bringing death instead of new life.

Yet, I'm such a superstitious man, I believe that neither kind of rape can be performed without some sort of agreement between the participants.

The sexual rape is an act of forced penetration, where the woman is pierced. This piercing is very hard to accomplish, if she's not to any extent surrendering to it.

Of course, she doesn't surrender willingly. But somehow her muscles must — however minutely — be weakened by the distraction of surrender, for the piercing to be at all possible.

Ironically, the woman's main surrender may be a disbelief in her own powers.

Perhaps most women do it as a paying of ransom. They accept one tragedy, in order to avoid another of permanent effect — namely the kind of rape that is murder.

In murder, too, the victim must be pierced, somehow, for his life to emanate. Also this piercing demands some kind of surrender from the target, to be at all possible.

If the victim's lust for life was solid and without any flaw — then the bullet would miss, the knife would slip, the poison would immediately return the same way it entered.

Indeed, it's impossible to kill someone who does not at all want to die.

That's why some people tend to survive incidents, which are overwhelmingly likely to be fatal.

They step out unharmed from demolished cars, they crawl up from the water twenty-four hours after their boat was wrecked, and stand up after tumbling down a stairway of one hundred steps. It happens more frequently than chance alone allows for.

Not to mention how people can drive their cars for years, or be daring pedestrians in city traffic, or get heavily drunk thousands of times, without having any dangerous incidents at all. What spell protects them?

Lust for life.

It's not an unbreakable capsule. From time to time, in the grinding pains of life's many little wounds, in the fatiguing experience of day-to-day monotony, who doesn't occasionally want to die?

A murderer with a sense of timing would find his prey easily convinced.

Also, the very disappointment of finding oneself the target of such intent, discovering that one is so despised, or such an impenetrable obstacle in the route of another — that alone can enforce the wish.

If someone wants me dead so much that he

dares break the laws of both Heaven and Earth to have it done — why not let him? Why stand in his way?

Refusal would feel like a theft of sorts, as much as the act of murder does.

He wants to take my life and I want to keep it. What really gives me the right over him?

Thereby, we are content to become martyrs. If someone wholeheartedly wants me dead, then, alas, so be it!

For some reason, I have the impression that it's mostly the good guys who are willing to comply and die. The bad guys rarely do.

Those we find precious in life on earth seem to be the least attached to it, The ones chewing on it without any manners or willingness to share, they hold onto it with immeasurable force.

This is costly to our world — having so many nice persons quickly pass, while the deplorable ones remain, seemingly forever.

On the other hand, who is the better martyr? Men live for a short time only, but we are dead for very long.

Yes, the dead are so much more important than the living. Once dead, people are invincible. Their personalities do, through the thoughts and hands of the living, accomplish formidable feats.

Every man is a centre of mysterious forces, all of them released at the moment of his death. It's impossible to foresee or control the effects of this discharge.

The moment and manner of each man's death is far more important than any other event in his life — more significant, even, than the circumstances of his birth.

Again, this tells us that murder is a thing of magic.

While practicing the gracious Japanese martial art of Aikido, my authentic Japanese master told me many old tales and legends. Several of them concerned donating one's most precious belonging to one who claimed it.

Life is a strange possession. To be stolen or conquered, given freely or sold for some incomprehensible price:

Once it leaves its original owner, it exists no more. A most elusive treasure.

Yet, my Japanese master told me:

When murdered, as life leaves him, a holy man will in this moment bring bliss to his bane.

That's a strange reward for someone provoking the Gods. Still, this is the very essence of the Japanese martial arts and really a good strategy for survival:

Don't enter the duel with life dear to you. Give it up, and it will not accept to leave you.

Life is like any lover. Worship her, and she'll despise you. Neglect her, and she'll cling to you — for as long as it works.

My Japanese master led a life burdened by the supremacy of his predecessors, the ones living as well as those legendary. He tried and tried to be like the holy men of ancient times, but found it rather more complicated than telling their tales.

Thus, there was an intriguing ambiguity in his obsession with these tales of acceptance towards death. Telling his dedicated students of the martial arts that the supreme master gives bliss to his murderer, might be a bit demanding — almost a challenge.

As of yet, though, no one has complied.

This is the most intriguing of all the stories he told me:

An old man and his two sons had decided to leave all, their wives and homes, for a quest to find salvation.

After many years of travel and hardship they came to a high mountain, which was said to give bliss to those who climbed it.

Villagers at the mountain's foot assured them that the only thing one had to do was to climb to its top, where a certain flower grew, then pick that flower and eat it.

Well, the father and his two sons began their march immediately, and it was an ordeal of unforeseen proportion. By every step they took, the wind grew stronger and the temperature dropped.

Finally, at the very brim of their endurance, they reached the top and found the flower growing there, its stalk sticking up through the snow. It was a strange kind of flower, dark in colors and with a forceful scent. They sat down to eat it, but the father hesitated.

What kind of plant, he wondered, could this really be? Looking like nothing else and smelling like nothing else, it was not a flower he'd like to have growing in his own garden.

So he told his younger son to taste it first, handing it over to him.

The boy obeyed his father, but the moment his tongue touched the flower, he fell down on the snow and died.

Now the father grew very thoughtful, watching his dead son and pondering the legend of this mountain and its flower.

Could all the tales he'd heard, and all the villagers at the foot of the mountain, be so wrong? He had to make sure.

So, he told his older son to taste the flower. The son obeyed, carefully picking it up from his brother's chest.

The moment his lips touched the flower, he fell on his back and was dead.

The father stood up. He watched his two dead sons, his heart pounding and tears emerging from his eyes. Then he climbed down the mountain.

Reaching its foot, the old man turned to watch the peak, high above. There he saw his two sons, shimmering of light, rising through the air, into Heaven.

I think that this tale is as true to the essence of salvation as the onion is to this world we live in.

The core of life is nothing, and the essence of salvation, its very prerogative, is death. It's not for the living.

Again, reason to contemplate murder.

Should I be grateful to my murderer, if one appears, sending me to the divine domain? Should I search the world over for him, has he not yet appeared, or use all my viciousness to provoke my neighbors into giving birth to one?

Will the kind of Jesus, at the other side of the border, be cunning enough to see through such trickeries?

He probably will.

On the other hand, if I do my utmost to preserve and prolong my life, for the purpose that he will not accuse me of all too eagerly leaving it — isn't that, too, a mockery of his principles?

Man is banned by his awareness. He can do nothing, absolutely nothing, without being conscious of its implications and possible consequences. Therefore, we are never completely innocent.

And never guilty? Oh yes, ever guilty.

There's the everlasting aftertaste of one single bite of the legendary apple. A taste even bitterer than that of the telltale onion.

Awareness is an evil spiral, spinning without pause in our minds, from birth unto the moment of death. Perhaps also beyond.

No wonder, we sometimes wish so much for an end to arrive that we do our best to approach it.

There is some comfort in contemplating murder.

The American Indians had higher demands on life than we tend to do. Or did they love it too much to compromise about it?

When the white man needed his cotton to be picked, he first considered the red man for the job. There he was, nearby and in abundance.

Red man, though, was not readily convinced.

He would not develop proper skills for this work, and when his life was trapped in slavery, he preferred to leave it completely.

White man had no antidote to suicide. Although life can certainly be mastered by worldly powers, death cannot.

Forced to realize this, the white man had to bring the black man, all the way from Africa, to do the picking of the cotton.

By paying the ultimate price, the Indians won their precious freedom.

In another world, this sacrifice of one generation probably would have been rewarded to all the following. Here, it did not.

When the white man found no practical use for the Indians, he simply exterminated them. A glorious death, indeed, and one to stain all white men's consciences forever on. But still, death.

Will the kind of Jesus find it in his heart to forgive the Indians their suicide? I pray that he does. If not, what judgment is the white man to expect?

Perish the thought.

Well, I wonder if we do at all inherit the sins of our ancestors. Probably for as long as we enjoy the fruits thereof.

And we do.

Suicide can be of so many differing kinds, few of which being as grand and heroic as that of the Indians.

Experts say that most suicide attempts are not altogether sincere in intent. The wish of the one committing it is not to find death, but to bring attention to the circumstances of his life. It's a cry for assistance.

As such, it's also a threat, almost blackmail:

Help me, or next time around I'll do it for real — and then you're to blame!

They rarely do it for real, though. The attempts may be many and as alarming as the crescendo of a turbulent symphony — but a finale it is not.

In spite of this, attempted suicides may become failures in such an ironic way that they really do lead to death. A suicide that failed to fail.

However sad this mishap may be, it gives a certain relief to those left behind. But it's very rare.

This game of pretense seems to be far more popular among women than among men. How come?

Can it be that women often relate to life in more of a closed circuit, more matter-of-factly, than do most members of the opposite sex?

I have the impression that women rarely are as curious about the beyond as men often are. Consequently, if the possibility of an afterlife is of little concern to them, such women must see death as more of a threat, a thing of horror. Unlife.

Accordingly, a suitable instrument for blackmail.

Women who are less attracted by death seem to show it less respect. They don't hesitate to play with it, like someone not really believing in it.

But they do believe in it. Death itself is much more real to them than to men. It's the beyond that is not. Death is just one thing — unlife. Not at all attractive.

It could very well have something to do with the experience of pregnancy. Being the melting pot of new life, it's hard to engage in fancy dreams about unlife.

A lady I know was constantly trying to kill herself, when in her mid-twenties. Mostly she used pills, not always of a kind that could be fatal in any reasonable dosis. It also happened that she slashed her wrists.

She always called somebody up, immediately after the drastic step. Although it caused a few hearts to speed up their beats for the rest of the night, she wasn't ever close to the point of no return.

The doctors held her for a few days at the hospital, then diagnosed her as healthy as can be and mildly but firmly showed her to the door.

I think the doctors didn't take her very seriously. They did not even insist on sending her to some kind of therapy. Well, they probably had the experience to tell the difference between her exercises and the real thing.

Still, it did become a strain on her friends. Her phone calls were received with very ambiguous emotions.

Given time, the very frequency of it could probably have killed her. At least, all those pills might have ruined her liver, had she not quit after a few years.

What happened?

She found a man, who made her pregnant.

Starting up another human life made her cease to wish for her own life to end. The baby ignited certain instincts inside of her and she forgot all about suicide. Along with the child arrived some kind of meaning to her life.

What better meaning could there be to a person's life than the life of another?

To make sure, she quickly repeated the cure. Today the two children take up all her time and energy. They're good at that.

What will happen when they have reached

the age where her assistance is no longer essential to them, I don't know. Yet another?

Or maybe she has come to the conclusion that she never really wanted to die in the first place. Her attempts were solely reactions against life. Death had nothing to do with it.

Those who really wish to die, on the other hand, show greater accuracy and competence. The manner of their voyage varies, but they usually succeed to depart.

Still, their action can be just as much directed to the world they leave, as is the action of those who never really plan to leave at all.

Often, their suicide is an accusation, intended for their blood to stain as large an area as possible.

They want their death to make such noise that its echo will forever ring in the ears of the poor ones left behind.

For some reason — maybe the inverted case of what goes for female suicidal behavior — this tends to be most popular among men.

I'm sure that they feel entitled to bring such punishment on those afflicted. Maybe they would often enough be acknowledged this right by anyone looking into the matter. Still, there seems to be an amount of narrow-mindedness involved.

Throwing oneself from the roof of an apartment building or in front of a train, or crashing one's car into a mountainside, tends to hurt other people entirely than those who could by the most farfetched of arguments deserve it.

It's odd how merciless those people can be, who claim to have been shown the least mercy. Were they really treated with all the negligence or cruelty for this rude farewell to be justified?

In my modest experience, those who suffered the most tend to be the least inclined to complain. Those who groan the loudest really seem to be the most privileged.

Pain must have its own law of relativity.

The most prolonged of suicides, also that which torments relatives and friends the worst, is drug abuse. All those hundreds of exotic narcotics, coming in every color and flavor, or plain old alcohol.

The addict may not always intend to have his excessive use end in death, neither consciously nor subconsciously — but mostly he does.

There's a T-shirt print popular in Sweden, telling it all:

"Booze slowly kills you — but who's in a hurry?"

If you wish to leave this planet, but are in no immediate hurry and don't mind terribly — maybe even enjoy — some serious humiliation and bodily decay along the way, then there's most certainly a drug for you.

Obviously, it's not the easy way out. Nor is it exactly a sign of cowardice. Sometimes, though, it can stem from indecision, or at least the lack of that overwhelming conviction.

Whatever the cause for this long and trying route, it tends to be unto others all that it is to the addict. One might even find it contagious, through the carrier of emotional attachment.

People who are strangely fond of addicts — and such people exist in at least the same abundance as addicts — tend to end up sharing also the addiction with them.

Might it actually be a wonderful way to go? Or is the explanation simply that the addict made the life of his loving one so miserable, the drug becomes her only consolation?

A risky business, indeed.

Five social workers in Sweden were involved in a long-time social project, where the aim was to cure one sole alcoholic. A middle-aged man, living in minute circumstances in the vicinity of Stockholm.

They worked very hard on it, all five of them, for three full years. Or was it three social workers on a five-year project? Somehow, the difference fails to strike me as all that significant.

Anyway, the drunkard did not get cured. Although the social workers sometimes succeeded to make him step out of the gutter and refuse the bottle for a while, he always fell back as soon as they removed their supporting arms.

Alcohol can be very persuasive, especially to someone with an ear for its kind of music.

When the time span of the project had elapsed, the social workers left to write a book about it.

Soon enough, the drunk killed himself — the fast way.

I'm not surprised. What was left for him to do?

Never again could he expect to receive the same attention. Never again would he be the centre, yes, the very source of income for a number of perfectly well established citizens.

When that spotlight of attention turned away from him, all was darkness.

Nobody really wants to leave kindergarten to stand on his own two feet.

Lots of people who get to re-experience the carefree existence of early childhood — in such places as prison cells or hospital beds — wish to remain right there forever.

In kindergarten you are taken good care of, with the big frightning world locked out and food being served at regular hours.

Who can blame them?

Some kinds of suicide I find sympathetic.

I heard that in the city of Gothenburg, at the southwest of Sweden, there is one method of voluntary passing on, which is incomparably the most popular among men. Gothenburg is a town of industry and shipping, not altogether unlike such places as Detroit in the USA and Liverpool in England.

This is the favorite type suicide of its male inhabitants:

When leaving home in the morning, the man intended on committing suicide brings the hose of his vacuum cleaner. After work, he buys the evening paper as usual and parks his car on some peaceful roadside out by the woods.

He attaches one end of the hose to the exhaust pipe and leads the other into a side window of the car. Then he relaxes on the driver's seat, leaves the motor running, reads the paper and slowly suffocates.

It's very neat, isn't it? Neat and clean.

Will the kind of Jesus appreciate this consideration towards posterity? Let's hope so.

Every suicide, though, as well as every murder, leaves a bitter taste in the mouths and guts of those left behind. Frustration. Death cannot be undone.

It's absolute. There we stand, all of us remaining, and can do nothing.

Nothing but pray — the very liturgy of the helpless. Pray for the departed one's happy arrival to the beyond, and pray for the rest of us to come to peace with the loss.

It's not only the kind of Jesus who accuses the one committing suicide. Posterity does, too.

Somehow, I have the impression that we'd like to accuse also those dead by the hands of others.

Yes, even to those who died of what is somewhat inadequately called the hand of fate, we wish to cry out:

How could you!

In whatever appearance, we do regard death as a crime, don't we?

That makes the death penalty a striking paradox. Punishing a crime with the most severe of crimes. It's rather absurd, proving again that we tend to regard ourselves as Gods.

It's particularly odd when the penalty is executed on a convicted murderer. To kill the murderer, punishing the criminal by repeating his crime, can that really be justified?

And is such a death at all a penalty?

What if there is such a thing as a glorious beyond? We know that life here on earth can become quite trying, especially for a murderer. Executing him may act as a quick relief.

Before the kind of Jesus, he will certainly be accused for his taking of a life, but must he not be shown some mercy because he was in his turn robbed of life? Maybe that evens up his heavenly account.

That is not the intention of our judicial system.

When a man commits murder, it's always regarded as a horrible crime. When it's done by society, the collective apparatus of man, it's called justice. I wonder, will the kind of Jesus agree?

Does he exclude this organized form of taking lives from blame?

If he doesn't, there will be a lot of people having a lot of explaining to do, when the time comes for that ultimate review.

There are several professions involved in the execution, participating more or less directly. I guess that the kind of Jesus doesn't slap only the hand that turned on the electricity or pulled the trigger or released the blade.

Or does he?

If not, things can become rather difficult. It does not take a superhuman stretch of the imagination to regard any one of a country's inhabitants, who doesn't protest against the death penalty, as partly guilty of every execution.

Are we?

The laws of man, tending to be more severe than we're led to believe that the divine ones are, would surely come to that conclusion if ever trying it in some kind of court. The divine perspective — being more complex and having a lot more information to consider — might see it differently.

Perhaps, in such a view, there's only one guilty, only one utterly responsible:

The executioner.

After all, his is the very hand without which there would be no officially inflicted murder. Who else, in this network of accomplices, is equally indispensable?

High authorities may decree this and that. The most impressive congregation of noblemen and sages may reach a most convincing verdict. Without someone to perform the punishment, nothing will happen.

Without the executioner there can be no execution, unless every condemned is as noble as ancient time Socrates, voluntarily emptying the cup of poison — whether or not he agrees with the judgment.

The samurai of old Japan often showed the same twisted self-discipline in *seppuku*, their ritual disembowelment. An obedient suicide.

Yet, their chosen method of departure was making a mess that could be meant as some criticism of the system. Watch me die, and think about it!

Society can afford many rebellions of that kind.

Anyway, this questionable heroism is rare. It takes an executioner to have others than the noblest among us leave this world upon command.

Without the acting force of the executioner,

the death penalty is no penalty at all. No judge
would be satisfied to pass the sentence of:
    "Death... please!"

So, the executioner is the force demanded by any court. He is the murderer of the murderer.

If he's not to argue for the court's wisdom being of a divine nature, and therefore of divine rights — then his sole defense is one, by which many questionable deeds have been and will be done:

"I was only doing my job."

That argument will hardly suffice in front of the very makers of the rules of life and death, namely the very makers of life and death.

He did his job, all right — but did he have to? There are other jobs.

Even if there were not, in the eyes of the divine he would do better to starve. By that he'd deserve pie in the sky when he died.

Is he not prepared to suffer the tough earthly consequences of being righteous, he must prepare for the consequences in the beyond.

Let's say that the executioner is the only person the Gods find guilty, and let's say — which I sincerely doubt — that the killing of some asocial individuals is essential to the well-being of all others.

I do doubt it. I mean — would the Gods create a world where it is necessary to break their primary rule?

Anyway, for the sake of argument, let's say that this is the case.

Then the executioner volunteers to be banned in the beyond. Therefore, by this formidable sacrifice, he is a veritable saint on earth. Hero among the living, and foe ever after.

Did he make a good bargain?

In truth, we human beings are so attached to each other, so passionately linked to our species, that most of us would gladly make the sacrifice of the executioner. To aid one's fellow beings, although by that becoming damned for eternity — what martyrdom can be grander?

It is so much easier to let oneself suffer every possible malice on earth, for what little time it lasts, when confident of praise in the eternity waiting up there.

Not that we can ever be confident about it, but some people claim that they are.

People who believe in the hereafter usually prepare for a pleasant stay in it. People who don't, they make the very most of what earthbound life can offer.

Must not the kind of Jesus find compassion for the one who knowingly deals himself the worst of hands?

They say that to judge, one needs to know all the circumstances. I'd say that if one does, judging may very well become impossible.

It surely takes a God to dare it, when considering the whole complexity of the situation. If divinity is any guarantee of the sentence being just — well, that remains to be seen.

Maybe the kind of Jesus avoids judgment on almost all felonies, not because of compassion, but from a sense of incompetence.

Another kind of socially sanctioned murder than the execution, and much more efficient, is war.

War has its own so-called ethics, by necessity being far more summary. The verdict is narrowed down to one single, decisive circumstance: the type of garment. Friend or foe — the book is judged by its cover. War is a clash of uniforms.

The excuse of the soldier, whatever rank, for participating in this formidable gluttony of ending people's lives is similar to that of a peacetime executioner:

"I only obeyed orders."

Like good watchdogs do.

Well, obedience, however neat, is not a carte blanche, neither for dogs nor men. Much less for men.

There is a choice — as always, it seems, in this universe of confusion. Unfortunately, there is a choice.

Although the price is high, many soldiers do choose to act in accordance with the most distant world. In war, Heaven is as distant as it can ever be.

Lots of soldiers refuse to obey, when ordered to shoot members of their own species because they are dressed in different garments. Not many enough, though. Not even nearly.

That morbid farce of the Vietnam War actually produced some appealing statistics. It seems that the soldiers of the US army shot some nine out of ten bullets high above the heads of the people with the wrong clothes, never at all intending to hit them.

No matter how sissy that might have made them feel at the occasion, I'm sure the remembrance will make them blush with pride, once they face the kind of Jesus.

The enemy didn't aim as high.

They had a reason, a motivation that the US soldiers were desperately lacking. But what will the conclusion be in the beyond? Will their reason suffice there, too?

The idea of defending one's land against intruders must be completely out of place in the domain that knows no nationalities and invites absolutely everybody.

Quite an amusing way for some soldiers to defend theirs deeds is:

"It was him or me."

The Gods would not hesitate the least to reply: "So what?"

You sacrifice someone else for yourself, or yourself for someone else. That's the arithmetic of it. Only somebody with the total conviction of a beyond could be blamed for choosing the latter.

On the other hand, if the soldier is certain of the heavenly laws, then he should be obliged to shoot, in order to deny himself the easy way out and not to make his fellow man a sinner.

Who wants to be a judge in Heaven?

Frankly, I don't really believe it's too much of a dilemma for the Gods to reach their verdict. They read not the circumstances involved in our actions, but simply the sincerity of our minds.

Our hearts, as we have it. They read what's in our hearts.

Whatever tangle the conscious mind makes of our thoughts and motivations, the degree of our sincerity is always evident to the Gods.

Mortals can't read such intricate diagrams with much reliability, if at all. We have to stick to the less disputable facts of circumstance. The who-dunit of the event, for starters. Followed by the more or less inspired guesswork as to why.

That's not easy to consider.

When we can safely claim to know the factual circumstances beyond any reasonable doubt, still the judgment demands a prodigious capacity of the mind. We're hardly ever that sure about the facts.

When judging murder, we take into consideration the concept of differing degrees of malice. We regard killing differently, depending on the method as well as the motif.

There's manslaughter, crime of passion or in sudden anger, and calculated homicide — also a number of nuances in between them.

In self-defense and acts of confusion, the murderer is said to be less responsible for his action. When calculated well in advance, it's regarded as particularly fiendish.

Is all that really relevant?

Somebody I know had an accident when he was in his late teens.

Together with two friends, he was strolling, late at night, through the suburban area where they lived. It was in the winter, between Christmas and New Year. Snow covered the ground. Most of the apartment building windows were dark and the air carried few sounds.

They were approached by a drug addict, some five years their senior, who was obviously high on something or other. Soon enough, they were involved in an intense quarrel, in the midst of which the addict pulled a knife.

One of the three youngsters succeeded in kicking the knife from his hand, another one grabbed it and in the unfortunate confusion threw it to the third of them.

The moment he held it securely in his hand, he rushed forward and stabbed the drug addict in the chest. Seven times.

The man died on the spot.

They ran away, but within twenty-four hours the police had them all arrested and the whole thing was brought to court.

The facts were obvious enough — who killed whom and why and such. But the court's considerations were more complex.

First of all, it was sort of self-defense. Sort of, in so much as the first stabbing could easily be explained by it, and maybe the second. But all seven? Hardly.

Then they found something out:

The defendant suffered from diabetes. Doctors explained that somebody with this malady might be overcome by an uncontrollable rage, when put in a situation of great stress.

Therefore, he must not be regarded as responsible for his deed. He was acquitted and sent to psychiatric care for observation and treatment. After a few months he was back home.

He has been doing fine since.

In fact, his companions at the night of the stabbing seem to have been more affected by it. I get the impression that they've had more severe struggles with their consciences than he ever did.

Still:

If the court is only to find the proper punishment for someone ending the life of another — must not the moral conclusion always be the same? Either it's wrong to kill or it's not.

If it's wrong, then there should be just one punishment for it, the same for every circumstance — simply because the crime is the same.

For the victim, anything else is an insult.

Of course, the court has got nothing to do with ethics and punishment. That's just a game we play.

Killing is not regarded as immoral. It's not that easy. This is obvious in the case of the executioner and the soldier. Like in so many cases of human law, the decisive issue is not the 'what', but the 'who' — concealed behind a 'why'.

The real aim of the legal system is not the right of the victim, but the comfort of everybody else — especially those who made and uphold the laws.

We seek no way to avenge the dead, may he rest in peace, but to protect the living.

That is what the court really has to consider, although the game of pretense sometimes confuses matters.

For example, in the case of the diabetic I guess that the court was somewhat overcome by the game of pretense, when releasing someone who could very well have another outburst of the same kind.

Maybe they thought that he'd only be a risk to drug addicts and such. The dispensable ones. And only when provoked.

Vengeance is not a human responsibility. We're told that the Gods want revenge to be their exclusive right. We comply, although maybe more out of comfort than obedience.

We pluck the weeds in our garden, not for the sake of the weeds, but for the sake of the roses. What more can we do than cultivate our garden?

Not even that do we handle very well.

We were not set out to be judges. Who can possibly cast the first stone?

Still, lots of people are being stoned. I wonder how.

Most certainly a ludicrous hypothesis, nevertheless lucrative, is the idea of a universe without Gods. A heaven of nothing but troposphere, stratosphere, mesosphere, ionosphere, and then vacuum.

I know that such a concept is preposterous, but still, let us ponder it for a moment. I'll try to make the moment as brief as the subject deserves.

If there is no God and no other afterlife than the wandering of molecules from one animal, through soil and plants, into the next — will the laws of life and death change? Will the ethics of, say, murder differ?

No.

Although no more needs to be said on the matter I'm compelled, by the very solace of this line of reasoning, to caress it a bit further with my words.

The laws of Heaven and Hell, of good and bad, would not change in the least — and here's why:

What's best for the Gods, whether they are real or not, is best for men also. What Heaven wishes is the ultimate choice for Earth.

Yes. If we could only comply with the intentions of Heaven, without any trickery or selfishly twisted interpretations, then Earth would soon become a place not the least bit inferior to it.

Accordingly, maybe Heaven is nothing but the ultimate utopian vision of the world we live in. And the laws of the Gods are not a system of merits for the dead, but a do-it-yourself guide for making Utopia come true in the world of the living.

We only have to read and apply the guide properly, for all of us to arrive there shortly.

I believe it will happen. I pray it will.

Bear with me, please, as I need to repeat:

What's best for the Gods, whether they exist or not, is best for men also.

Could we only comply with the intentions of Heaven, without any trickery or selfishly twisted interpretations — and history tells us that this is a most difficult task — then Earth would soon become a place not the least bit inferior to it.

Yes, maybe divine law is a do-it-yourself guide for making Utopia come true.

Utopia. Wouldn't that be nice?

Strangely, some say not.

We often joke about Heavenly things, claiming them to be utterly naive. A Paradise on earth, we say, would really be a bore.

Nonsense.

Certainly, our concept of Hell is usually far more exciting than that of Heaven.

Like the Disney movie *Fantasia*, where the Devil appears in fiery splendor, surrounded by hordes of naked men and women involved in quite intriguing perversions. The cinema house is filled with thunderous music.

The Heavenly domain, on the other hand, is depicted by a serene line of grayish monks, walking through a gloomy countryside, accompanied by sleepy music. Each of the identical little monks carries a candle, which doesn't help much against the spiritual dusk of the scene.

If that's the case, if that's a relevant description of Heaven and Hell, then who wouldn't choose to spend eternity in the lower quarters?

But it's not.

Honestly — what could you expect from Disney?

Bliss is what it is, infinitely incomparable. Beyond words, beyond any worldly form of description. Hell is not.

That's the catch. Just like a world of heroes and their martial quests, Hell makes better cinema. But that's its only advantage.

Heaven is something else.

You know, don't you?

At some time, we've all had a taste of it. That, the Gods — the elusive ones — do grant us. One taste of Heaven and sweet bliss.

Wherever and whenever it strikes us, we are stunned. The rest of our lives, no matter how long, will differ from what they were like before that moment.

One such taste should suffice, wouldn't you say, for living in certainty of what to cherish and what not.

The problem of peace is somewhat similar to that of Heaven and Hell. It's almost a question of semantics:

The word *war* is filled with forceful meaning. Gory details and what the Hollywood movie industry calls special effects.

Peace, on the other hand, is merely a negation, a very passive thing. The way the word works in our minds, it could easily be substituted by 'un-war'. War and no war.

No wonder, peace finds it difficult to attract as soon as it isn't missing.

And no wonder, war becomes an obsession in the minds of both those who claim that it's needed, for one or other noble cause, and those who deplore it unconditionally.

Yes, it's an obsession of most minds as well as societies, the latter of which are in essence nothing but the manifestations of our minds.

We find it impossible, at length, not to indulge in war.

The Swedish organization of writers for peace — calling itself Writers Against Nuclear Arms, as if other ways of battle were harmless — once wanted to compose a book on the joy of peace. It was to work as an inspiration for the peace efforts, sort of a catalogue of the values of life unharmed by war.

A number of writers contributed with poems, short stories and such, where war was to be completely excluded. Only the priceless bliss of peace, in one or other aspect, was to be depicted.

I participated, too, I'm embarrassed to admit, with a short piece on the joy of waking up — a joy of sometimes ambiguous nature, of course, but always preferable to not waking up at all. Or so we see it, anyway.

Frankly, I have no idea what not waking up is like.

The project failed completely.
Without the contrasting side of war, no writer could bring attraction to his tale. I failed, too. I needed the contrast, although unspoken — of not waking up at all — to make the awakening sweet enough.

Artists, who were asked to illustrate the book, had immediately found the reason for this failure and therefore refused to participate in the first place.
It would be like trying to make a drawing in only white, they explained. No black at all. What kind of drawing would that be? For one thing, nobody would be able to see it.

They were wrong, as misled as Disney. Black is not war, not evil — nor is white necessarily good.
War is war. Peace is fabulous peace.
The failure of the writers was not the un-

avoidable consequence of a paradox. It was a failure of their insufficient artistry. Peace should not be judged by this. The writers, the poor guys, should.

Although we frequently forget, we are but human. Some artistic feats demand more than that.

The failure of the artists was not very different. By not even trying, but declaring it utterly impossible, they confessed to their ignorance of one essential thing, making all the difference in the world.

One thing, wherein the solution to this problem lies:

Beauty.

In beauty hides — yes, hides — the greatest attraction of peace. And beauty can be a spectacular special effect.

Isn't it strange, in a country that fought its last war way back at the beginning of the nineteenth century, that its artists should be unable to illustrate this fortunate circumstance?

No, it's not strange.

One of mankind's most tragic mechanisms is the limited time it's able to remember. Memories, no matter how horrid, tend to fade in mere years. Two centuries could make Doomsday itself fall into oblivion.

Regular human wars have much shorter life spans in the awareness of the human mind than the Armageddon would. We rapidly forget the torments of war and tend to long for something — anything — to take us out of the drab monotony of everyday life.

Soon enough, we get just that. Anything.

Only a fool would fail to sense, immediately and overwhelmingly, the splendor of the word *peace*. Only a complete fool would ever long for it to end.

A fool of that kind, though, needs not to feel lonesome.

There are many colorful aspects of murder, in a spectrum covering all nuances from the accidental manslaughter outside a bar at night, to the holocaust of modern warfare. The most impressive of murderers, though, and incomparably the most experienced, is nature itself.

That mother we call Nature, is an equally colossal donor and collector of lives — just as we'd like to regard ourselves.

While we must generally work like crazy to have life escape one single creature, Mother Nature simply shakes her body and, behold, thousands of lives are swept away.

Our bomb is mighty, all right, and makes devastating noise — but compared to even a modest size tornado, or the tsunami following an earthquake far from record level on the Richter scale, it's a petty thing.

In the perspective of such magnificence, we're still in kindergarten. Although we'd like to believe that we're advancing rapidly in our development, we've got a long way to go before we accomplish anything equally lethal.

Fortunately.

Murder seems to be what ecology is all about.

We're all mere hunters and prey, to eat or to be eaten. Nobody can escape these wildlife gladiator games. The rules of the games sure mock the one who nobly lowers his sword, just to be swiftly decapitated and served as his enemy's supper.

Were this sacrifice really the moral demand of the Gods, then they must have anticipated rapid extinction of those pure at heart — leaving the less compassionate beasts guilty and their bellies full.

No, it seems that the only moral limit the Gods put to this global system of murder, is to keep it out of the family. Don't kill within your own species.

Some people claim that the law should be more strict. Vegetarians often state that the reason for banishing all the fauna from their plates is the immorality of killing things alive. Creatures who live and feel pain should be spared.

Well, wouldn't that include plants as well?

They live, for sure, which is proven by their decay when not sufficiently watered. After attaching them to — of all things — lie detectors, some say that plants perceive their surroundings and feel pain, just like animals do.

Maybe the only difference between flora and fauna is the manner in which they communicate. For one thing, plants are much slower.

If plants are just as much alive as animals, then a noble being should exclude them, too, from his menu. By this line of reasoning, though, his diet would become meager.

Fruits would be acceptable. They are what plants produce just for the purpose of others eating them — as long as the nuts are not consumed.

No nut, no core.

The idea of living on nothing but fruits is amiable, but is it adequate nutrition? Furthermore, if this diet becomes widespread among us, wouldn't we soon be forced to breed those plants as violently as we now do with animals, crops, and vegetables, just to make their fruits suffice?

Why can't we live on sunshine alone? After all, it's only a question of energy.

What goes for the universe as a whole, that the sum of energy must always be the same, is equally true for man. What energy I consume, by keeping my temperature and walking about, I have to win back. Where I take my energy from — that's of no importance.

The prospect of living on pills, vitamins and proteins purely factory-made, is not altogether disgusting. Living without needing to kill, just by mixing this and that chemical substance. Artificial, we call it, as if it had not been extracted from nature. Why not? Maybe one day we will.

Still, murder will not be gone from the face of the earth. No, the least cooperative of all murderers remains. Who is that?

God, of course.

The intricate biological machinery of man really allows for a longevity we hardly reach.

All the body cells, except those of the nervous system, are renewed in such a fashion that every seven years the body is completely reconstructed. Replaced from top to bottom.

So, the only irreparable things in the whole body are the nerves and the brain cells. Still, they would suffice for much longer than the hundred or so years optimally given us.

Scientists are puzzled. Why do we grow old? Why the ageing process, not at all called for?

No matter how careful we are with our diets, nor how much we protect our bodies with medicine and physical exercises — by time, our automatic decay is commenced, always with fatal outcome.

Gods lure behind this. Murder of a divine proportion.

They have decided that we should walk on earth for a limited time, and then — whatever we do, whatever we may feel about it — life is gradually stolen from us, sucked from our very chests.

It's not done without some effort on their behalf, though. We human beings rarely give away our most priced possession freely, especially not to such elusive entities as the Gods.

They have to fight for it.

In many cases the fight is so uneven, it takes little more than one piercing of the heart for a definite outcome. But sometimes the Gods must roll up their sleeves and use every trick in the book.

I'm sure that with some people who have walked this planet, it must have been quite a costly victory.

Knowing all, the Gods ought to be aware and wary of this. When it comes to the most difficult ones of us, the Gods seem to prepare for the final battle by starting it very early. Sometimes they do it already at certain men's very moment of arrival to this world.

I have friends who are deeply afflicted by such divine precautions. They are strong-willed and enchanted by life. Fate hits them with many a forceful blow.

The divine intention with this constant misfortune must be to make them fatigued, when the time comes. It is to weaken their resistance.

Indeed, I suspect that the Gods utilize this method, more or less, on each and every one of us. Life isn't permitted to be all pleasure, so as not to make us too attached to it.

Could that be the explanation to all the pain going on — a measure of precaution?

Still, a few of us stand up from every blow, stronger than before. Yes, some people sure are a match for the Gods.

Yet, they always win in the end.

Every man's life, no matter how dear to him, is finally conquered and ended. Each proud neck will bend and every firm grip will eventually slip.

Why are the Gods unbeatable?

Simply because they will not cease until they win. Time's on their side. That is — even to the Gods — a most powerful ally.

They have a lot of time.

Well, that's not the whole truth. They find one more accomplice. Another aid in their feat, and the crucial one: the accordance of the victim.

As in every murder, no matter what giant holds the blade, the victim must — whether ardently or infinitesimally — allow it.

By time we do quite willingly let our lives be stolen. Even the most passionate, the most euphorically vivid ones do.

Although miraculous, life does by time become a bit boring or at least fatiguing. Not in the cells of our bodies, perhaps, though they tend to lose their vigor, but in our minds — the very substance that is never renewed.

So, one day, we lean back and expose our necks, overcome by the sentiment that now it may very well suffice.

Even of the best of meals one can only eat so much. Although we still regard it as very tasty, indeed, we push the plate away and close our mouths.

Then the Gods are free to do their burglary.

It hits me — maybe that's the sole reason for the Gods' intolerance towards murder among men. They want that pleasure reserved for themselves.

There is pleasure at both sides of the dagger. On the one hand, the excitement of the person who performs the stabbing, stemming from the satisfaction of doing the irreversible. On the other hand, the relief of the person being stabbed, thereby leaving this earthly existence in one of the rare ways that will cause no embarrassment at all in front of the kind of Jesus.

Great pleasure.

I guess that if applied at the right moment, murder can be an almost ecstatic form of intercourse between the two participants — or masturbation, in the case of suicide.

In the words of Juliet, the young girl who loved so much and strongly that it would be impossible to settle down in a lifelong marriage:

"Oh, happy dagger!"

Why does she speak so to the only one involved, who doesn't enjoy the deed? Or does she?

Maybe the instrument, although having no say of its own in this, is as pleased as the others involved. Who can say that the tool will not derive any satisfaction from participating? To be the instrument, without which the murder would not take place, and yet to be innocent of it.

That's really not so different from the role of the executioner, except for his ability of a choice.

What is the experience, if any, of the instrument?

Well, in truth, when every aspect is considered, isn't that what we all are? Gods and men, as well as those objects claimed to have no soul:

Mere instruments.

Maybe once, the Gods were really the initiators. The omnipotent and capricious rulers of the game. But now, after eons of complex inter-action, they must be as indistinguishably in-volved as the rest of us.

We're all doing what we must, allowed but one choice: to enjoy it, like good sports, or to suffer and complain at each moment.

What choice is that?

Yes, occasionally I contemplate murder. But do I consider it?

No.

I need not. Enough of it, as it is. Come shout with me:

Enough!

Epilogue

Although I'm a Swedish author, I wrote the first version of *Occasionally I contemplate Murder* in English. That was in an attempt to find a lightness of language to contrast the somber theme of the book. The Swedish language is prone to Midwinter gloom and deep forest shadows.

I didn't really know what to do with the finished manuscript, when the brilliant poet and publisher Eric Fylkesson wanted to read it, and then to publish it in Swedish. I told him that I doubted whether it would at all be possible to find the right lighthearted language for it in Swedish, but when I commenced the translation I found that it worked like a charm.

Because of the English original, I was able to find the tone also in Swedish.

Now, the world is smaller and books penetrate every border. It is time for Murder to be published in its original language.

Let me tell you why I wrote it:

As a novelist, I had initially found that writing stories was a good way of getting my thoughts and messages across. But by time I found that stories could also be an easy way out, a substitute for content instead of a carrier of it.

So, I wanted to test myself: did I have something to say, really? Would there be any substance visible, without a story to imply it?

This book was the test. You be the judge.

Malmö in October 2006,
Stefan Stenudd

Welcome to my website:
www.stenudd.com